C.1

EXPLORING SCIENCE

METAMORPHIC ROCKS

RECYCLED ROCK

BY DARLENE R. STILLE

Content Adviser: Lynn S. Fichter, Ph.D.,
Department of Geology/Environmental Science, James Madison University

Science Adviser: Terrence E. Young Jr., M.Ed., M.L.S.,
Jefferson Parish (Louisiana) Public School System

Reading Adviser: Rosemary G. Palmer, Ph.D.,
Department of Literacy, College of Education, Boise State University

Compass Point Books · Minneapolis, Minnesota

Compass Point Books • 3109 West 50th Street, #115 • Minneapolis, MN 55410

This book was manufactured with paper containing
at least 10 percent post-consumer waste.

Photographs ©: Corbis/Charles Mauzy, cover; Corbis/Bernard Annebicque, 4; Shutterstock/Kim Pin Tan,
5; Photo Researchers, Inc./Wayne Scherr, 7; Photo Researchers, Inc./Michael P. Gadomski, 9; Lynn
Fichtels, 10, 28; Corbis/Ludovic Maisant, 12; Photo Researchers, Inc./Cordelia Molloy, 13; Shutter-
stock/Rodolfo Arpia, 15; Corbis/Jim Sugar, 16; Photo Researchers, Inc./Science Source, 17; Photo
Researchers, Inc./Kenneth Murray, 18; Corbis/Ric Ergenbright, 20; Photo Researchers, Inc./Dr Jer-
emy Burgess, 24; Corbis/Richard T. Nowitz, 26; Photo Researchers, Inc./John Kaprielian, 29; Photo
Researchers, Inc./Fletcher & Baylis, 30; Shutterstock/Lagui, 32; Photo Researchers, Inc./Biophoto
Associates, 33; Photo Researchers, Inc./A. B. Joyce, 34; Corbis/M. Angelo, 35; Photo Researchers,
Inc./Gregory G. Dimijian, M.D., 36; Photo Researchers, Inc./Kaj R. Svensson, 37; Corbis/WildCoun-
try, 39; Shutterstock/Kaspars Grinvalds, 40; Shutterstock/Cecilia Lim H M, 41; Corbis/Richard
Klune, 42; Shutterstock/Bobby Deal/RealDealPhoto, 43; Shutterstock/Michael Fuery, 44; Shut-
terstock/Joe Gough, 46.

Editor: Anthony Wacholtz
Designer: The Design Lab
Page Production: Lori Bye
Photo Researcher: Lori Bye
Illustrator: Ashlee Schultz

Creative Director: Keith Griffin
Editorial Director: Nick Healy
Managing Editor: Catherine Neitge

Library of Congress Cataloging-in-Publication Data
Stille, Darlene R.
  Metamorphic rocks : recycled rock / by Darlene R. Stille ; illustrator,
Ashlee Schultz.
      p. cm.—(Exploring science)
  Includes index.
  ISBN 978-0-7565-3255-0 (library binding)
  1. Rocks, Metamorphic—Juvenile literature. I. Schultz, Ashlee, ill.
  II. Title. III. Series.
  QE475.A2S79 2008
  552'.4—dc22   2007032682

Visit Compass Point Books on the Internet at www.compasspointbooks.com
or e-mail your request to custserv@compasspointbooks.com

About the Author

Darlene R. Stille is a science writer and author of more than 80 books
for young people. When she was in high school, she fell in love with
science. While attending the University of Illinois, she discovered that
she also loved writing. She was fortunate enough to find a career as
an editor and writer that allowed her to combine both of her interests.
Darlene Stille lives and writes in Michigan.

TABLE OF CONTENTS

CHAPTER ONE

What Is Metamorphic Rock?

IN 1498, MICHELANGELO BUONARROTI, a young Italian artist in Rome, was hired by a Roman Catholic cardinal, a high church official, to create a religious sculpture. The sculpture was to be a life-size *Pieta*, a representation of Jesus being cradled by his mother after the crucifixion.

Michelangelo went to the rock quarries around the city of Carrara in northern Italy. There he selected a big block of marble more than

Michelangelo's *Pieta* was one of his earliest works. It helped establish his reputation as a talented artist and sculptor.

6 feet (2 meters) long and 5 feet (1.5 m) high. For two years, Michelangelo hammered, drilled, and polished his block of metamorphic rock until the work was completed. His *Pieta* became one of the most famous sculptures in the world. Michelangelo became one of the greatest artists of all time, and today his *Pieta* is on display at St. Peter's Basilica at the Vatican in Rome.

Many statues carved out of marble were used to adorn St. Peter's Basilica.

Michelangelo chose marble, one of many kinds of metamorphic rock, for this and other sculptures. Metamorphic rock is one of three main types of rock found on Earth. Metamorphic rock forms from the other two types of rock: igneous and sedimentary. New kinds of metamorphic rock can even form from other metamorphic rocks. The word *metamorphic* comes from Greek words meaning "to change form."

ROCKS ARE NOT FOREVER

Solid rock that makes up mountains, cliffs, statues, and monuments looks as though it should last forever. But rock is always changing. Rocks can stay the same only if the conditions on Earth that formed them stay the same.

However, conditions on Earth, and Earth itself, are always changing. The rocks that make up Earth changes with them. Knowing how igneous and sedimentary rocks form can help in understanding how rocks can change by metamorphosis.

Igneous rocks form from rocks that are so hot that they melt. Below ground, the melted rock is called magma. Magma in the mantle is a mixture of many kinds of minerals. When the minerals in the magma cool, they form rocks. What type of rock they form depends on the minerals and how quickly the magma cools.

Melted rock that comes out of a volcano is called lava. As the melted rock cools, it becomes solid, igneous rock. An igneous rock, such as granite or basalt, seems hard, tough, and indestructible. On Earth's surface, however, an igneous rock is unstable. An igneous rock that lies on the ground for thousands of years is attacked by wind, water, and gases in the atmosphere. This attack is called weathering.

Forces of nature such as wind and water break off pieces of rock from a cliff or mountain, creating a unique design.

Igneous rock, like all rock, is made up of minerals. Physical weathering breaks the rock into smaller and smaller pieces. For example, blowing winds and driving rain can break down the granite rock of a mountain into pieces of gravel and sand. Each piece contains the same minerals. Quartz is a common mineral in granite, so the weathered sand grains will also contain quartz. Chemical weathering occurs when minerals dissolve in water flowing over or dripping on rock. Chemicals in the water cause the rock minerals to change. For example, carbon dioxide in water reacts with the mineral feldspar to create minerals that form clay.

Rivers and streams carry the smaller pieces of rock—such as sand, silt, and clay—downhill. On the bottoms of lakes and oceans, they become sediments. Layer after layer of sediments build up over millions of years. The weight of all the layers causes tremendous pressure. The pressure packs the sediments so tightly together that they form layers of rock.

EARTH RECYCLES ROCKS

The only place on Earth that you will find the sediments that make up sedimentary rock is on the planet's surface. You will find sedimentary rock on hills, plains, and the bottom of the sea. As more and more sediment piles up on the seafloor, however, it buries older rocks deeper and deeper below the

surface. Eventually these rocks may be buried miles below the surface. Down there, conditions are very different from those on the surface of Earth.

The deeper you go into Earth, the hotter it gets. Deep in the mantle, the pressure also gets higher and higher. Rocks get hot enough to melt and become igneous rocks. Sedimentary

Outcroppings of the metamorphic rock schist along the Susquehanna River in Pennsylvania

rocks that formed from igneous rocks become igneous rocks again. The slow change from one rock form to another as conditions change is called the rock cycle.

Between the mild conditions at Earth's surface and the tremendous temperatures and pressures in the mantle, rocks undergo many other changes. These changes are called metamorphic changes, and they form metamorphic rock. Heat, pressure, or chemicals in hot water can cause metamorphism. Sometimes only one condition, such as heat, causes

Eclogite is a green metamorphic rock with traces of garnet. It often comes from part of an oceanic crust that subducted, or forced below another part of the crust, and then returned to the surface.

metamorphic changes. Sometimes two or more of these conditions cause the rock to change.

Metamorphic rock can then be weathered to form particles
of sediment that become sedimentary rock. In this way, the
rock cycle continues. The sedimentary rock that has formed
from weathered metamorphic rock melts in the mantle and
then hardens into igneous rock. The rock cycle begins anew.

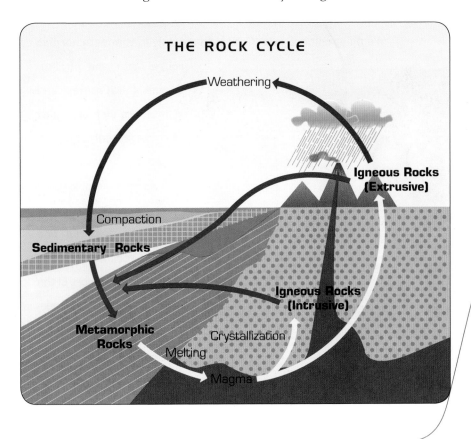

THE ROCK CYCLE

Weathering

Igneous Rocks
(Extrusive)

Compaction

Sedimentary Rocks

Igneous Rocks
(Intrusive)

Metamorphic
Rocks

Crystallization

Melting

Magma

Metamorphic Rock Minerals

All rocks are made up of minerals. A mineral is a natural, nonliving, solid material. Each mineral is made of one or more chemical elements. An element is a substance that contains only one kind of atom.

Although geologists have found about 3,000 minerals on Earth, only about 100 are common in rocks. Metamorphic rocks contain many minerals not found in other rocks. For example, chlorite is a mineral found only in the metamorphic rocks slate and phyllite.

Garnet, staurolite, and kyanite are also examples of minerals only found in metamorphic rocks.

As metamorphic rocks move through the rock cycle, they heat up and begin to reach the melting point. More and more of the minerals in the metamorphic rock change into those found in igneous rock, such as quartz, feldspar, biotite, and amphibole.

Red garnet stones are often used in jewelry. Garnet is the January birthstone.

Plate Movements and Metamorphic Rock

THE ROCK CYCLE is driven by the movements of more than 20 gigantic plates. The plates make up Earth's crust—the thin, hard outer layer of Earth. Under the crust are two more layers: the mantle and the core. Temperatures in the mantle are high enough to melt rock and form magma.

The huge plates, called tectonic plates, float and move around on the molten rock of the mantle. In some places on Earth, the plates crash together. Sometimes the edge of one colliding plate slides beneath another plate and melts because of the heat inside Earth. Sometimes edges of colliding plates fold and bend upward, causing mountain ranges to form. In other places, the plates pull apart.

All these conditions produce certain kinds of igneous, sedimentary, and metamorphic rocks that are unique to each set of plate conditions.

A rift valley in Iceland was created as two tectonic plates moved apart.

Every rock forms in certain places on Earth for a specific reason. This reason is related to the motion of the plates. Geologists call this motion plate tectonics. The relationship between plate tectonics and the rocks that form as a result allow geologists to figure out what Earth was like millions of years ago.

The moving together or pulling apart of tectonic plates enables molten rock in the mantle to form igneous rock. Where two plates are pulling away from each other, openings called volcanic vents form. Magma rises to the surface through the volcanic vents and cools to form rock that makes new crust. Such vents are usually in the ocean floor. For example, two plates are moving apart in the middle of the Atlantic Ocean, creating vents in the ocean floor.

Over millions of years, the slowly moving plates that carry the seafloor and its sedimentary rock can plunge beneath a colliding plate and melt. When the edge of one plate plunges under the other plate, the sedimentary rock melts as it goes deeper into the hot Earth and becomes magma. When the magma rises to the surface and cools, it forms igneous rock.

DID YOU KNOW?

Tectonic plates move approximately 4 inches (10 centimeters) a year—about as fast as human hair grows.

MAGMA AND METAMORPHISM

Where the edge of one colliding plate slides under another, magma often rises. The plate that carries the Pacific Ocean, for example, is sliding under the plate that carries North America. The magma melts the cooler rock above and around it as it rises higher and higher through the crust. As the magma burns through existing rock in the plate, it creates volcanoes.

Geologists call the existing rock the parent rock or country rock. Rising magma can form huge underground

The cliffs of Catalina Island in California are made of the metamorphic rock blueschist. It morphed from shale, leading scientists to believe that Catalina Island was once part of a subduction zone.

pools called batholiths. It can rise to the surface through a pipelike vent in a volcano and erupt as lava. The heat from magma underground in a batholith or volcanic vent can bake the parent rock and change it into metamorphic rock. Lava flowing onto the surface can heat the rock on the ground and change it into metamorphic rock.

MOUNTAINS AND METAMORPHISM

Some individual mountains form when lava from a volcanic vent cools to form igneous rock. The igneous rock then builds up into a mound or cone shape. Japan's Mount Fuji is a volcanic mountain, and the Hawaiian Islands are the tops of volcanic mountains. Magma that stays below the surface cools to form big mounds called dome mountains.

Lava can reach temperatures of 2,192 degrees Fahrenheit (1,200 degrees Celsius), approximately 12 times as high as the boiling point of water.

Black Smokers

Far below the ocean surface, there is a world where inky, black "clouds" boil out of vents, or cracks, in the seafloor. These clouds are fountains of hot water that carry chemicals up from rocks far below. Magma heats water that has seeped down through the rocks. Like water filtering through coffee grounds, the hot water dissolves minerals out of the rock. The minerals contain sulfur, a chemical that creates the black color. New rock forms from minerals in the water and builds up around the vents to form tall "chimneys." This process is called hydrothermal metamorphism. It changes basalt, the igneous rock commonly found on the seafloor, into soapstone and serpentine. The hot water also deposits metals, such as gold and copper.

Strange forms of life, such as tube worms and mussels, also exist around black smokers. There is no light that deep in the ocean, meaning there are no plants, which depend on energy from the sun. Instead, the tube worms and mussels eat bacteria that survive on the sulfur coming out of the deep-sea vents.

The water around black smoker vents can range from 660 to 840 F (350 to 450 C).

Most mountains form because of the movement of tectonic plates. The collision of plates creates mountain ranges and mountain belts. A range is a grouping of mountains, such as the Rocky Mountains in the western United States. A mountain belt is a grouping of mountain ranges. The Appalachian Belt in the eastern United States includes the White Mountains, Green Mountains, Catskills, and Blue Ridge Mountains. The Alps are a mountain belt in Europe, and the Himalayas, with the tallest mountains in the world, are in Asia.

Hard rocks at Earth's surface become soft during metamorphism. These rocks can fold into strange shapes, such as the rocks in the Shining Rock Wilderness in North Carolina.

The edges of the great plates that formed these mountains folded up when the plates collided in the same way the fenders of a car crumple after an accident. These folds look like gigantic waves in the rock. The force of the collision created great pressure that made cracks in the crust called faults.

The tremendous pressure caused by the plates pushing against one another caused the sedimentary and igneous rocks to change into metamorphic rocks. The bases of the mountains are made mostly of metamorphic rock. In addition, moving plates cause friction along faults. The friction creates heat that can cause metamorphic changes in the rock.

The mountains that make up the Himalayas cover 1,500 miles (2,400 kilometers) across southern Asia.

Making Rocks Morph

METAMORPHISM TAKES PLACE because of three conditions: pressure, temperature, and chemicals in hot fluids. The weight of rock pressing on other rock increases pressure. When sediments build up in rock layers, the weight of the layers on top increases the pressure on the layers below. Pressure also increases when plates collide. The edges of the plates crumple up. The collision puts great

The Painted Hills, which were created by a buildup of sedimentary rock layers, are part of the John Day Fossil Beds National Monument in Oregon.

pressure on the rocks that make up the edges of the plates.

Temperatures in rock can increase in several ways. Heat inside Earth can heat layers of sedimentary rock that have been pressed downward by many layers of rock above. Because friction creates heat, rocks that rub together as two plates move past one another heat up. Collisions also create heat. Two plates moving together sometimes collide head-on

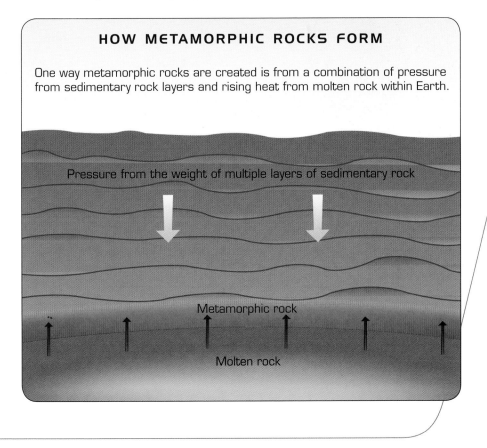

HOW METAMORPHIC ROCKS FORM

One way metamorphic rocks are created is from a combination of pressure from sedimentary rock layers and rising heat from molten rock within Earth.

Pressure from the weight of multiple layers of sedimentary rock

Metamorphic rock

Molten rock

at a very slow pace, bending and folding the rock. Energy from the collision changes to heat energy in the rocks.

Hot water picks up chemicals from surrounding rock. The type of chemicals the water picks up depends on the minerals in the rock that it passes over and through.

TYPES OF METAMORPHISM

Certain combinations of heat, pressure, and hot fluids cause particular types of metamorphism. Geologists have identified five kinds of metamorphism. The two major types seen at Earth's surface—not counting the ocean floor—are contact metamorphism and Barrovian metamorphism.

Contact metamorphism occurs when magma rises to the surface. Often times, the rising magma forms a volcano. In contact metamorphism, temperatures are very high but pressure is low. For heat to create metamorphic rock, the temperature must be from 392 to 2,192 F (200 to 1,200 C). Temperatures lower than this are not high enough to cause changes in existing rock.

Temperatures greater than 2,192 F will melt the existing rock to form magma. The hot magma melts the cooler parent rock above and around it as it rises higher and higher through the crust. Close to the magma, temperatures are high enough to bake the rock that does not melt. At these temperatures, just beneath the melting point of the existing rock, metamorphic rock forms. The most common rocks formed by contact metamorphism are hornfels, quartzite, and marble.

Barrovian metamorphism occurs over a large area. This type of metamorphism is sometimes called regional metamorphism. It occurs because of varying temperatures and pressures. The heat can come from a large mass of rising magma or from rock being pressed down into the mantle. The

Stratified quartzite in Australia was created from the sedimentary rock sandstone.

pressure comes from colliding plates. Barrovian metamorphism occurs during mountain building, and it creates large deposits of metamorphic rocks. This type of metamorphism creates a wide range of metamorphic rocks, such as slate, phyllite, schist, gneiss, migmatite, quartzite, and marble.

Flat layers of slate are produced from heat and pressure acting on shale, clay, or other rocks.

> **DID YOU KNOW?**
>
> Ancient Egyptians carved boulders of gneiss into statues of pharaohs, or rulers.

Hydrothermal metamorphism is caused by hot water or other fluids that are carrying chemicals. Magma, for example, contains water that can seep into cracks in the country rock. Temperatures and pressures do not have to be very high for hydrothermal metamorphism to take place. Reactions between chemicals in the fluids and the parent rock result in new, metamorphic rock. The metamorphic rocks serpentine and soapstone, which form around black smokers, are created by hydrothermal metamorphism.

Two other types of metamorphism only take place deep in the upper layers of the mantle between 5 and 150 miles (8 and 240 km) below Earth's surface. Blueschist metamorphism occurs on the edge of a tectonic plate that is sliding under another plate. The sediments that are being dragged down are not very hot as the plate heads downward. The pressure, however, gets greater and greater. The high pressure causes a type of metamorphic rock called blueschist to form. The very high pressures in the mantle cause another metamorphic rock, eclogite, to form from two types of igneous rocks: basalt and gabbro. Geologists call this process eclogite metamorphism.

Limestone and Calcite

Limestone, the rock from which marble forms, is one of the best known sedimentary rocks. Calcite is the mineral that forms limestone. Seawater contains carbon dioxide and other chemicals needed to make calcite. Calcite layers formed at the bottom of ancient seas when the water evaporated millions of years ago.

Some calcite that formed limestone came from ancient sea creatures. The creatures took calcite out of seawater to make shells. After the creatures died, the calcite shells fell to the seafloor. On the bottom of the ocean, they formed sediment. The calcite layers were buried under layers of rock. The pressure created by the weight of the rock turned the calcite on the sea bottom into limestone.

Certain metamorphic conditions involving heat and pressure can cause limestone to morph into marble. Sometimes you can see the fossil shells of snails, ammonites, and other ancient life forms in a piece of marble.

A hill of calcite formed from minerals in the hot springs at Palette Springs in Yellowstone National Park.

METAMORPHIC GRADES

Because metamorphic rocks form over a range of temperatures and pressures, geologists use categories called metamorphic grades to describe the conditions under which they formed. The metamorphic grades are low, intermediate, and high.

Low-grade metamorphosis represents low pressures and temperatures just above 392 F (200 C). Slate and phyllite are low-grade metamorphic rocks. High-grade metamorphosis represents very high pressures and temperatures from 1,472 F (800 C) to just below melting. Gneiss is a high-grade metamorphic rock. Intermediate-grade metamorphosis rocks form at pressures and temperatures between those of low- and high-grade metamorphosis. Schist is an example of an intermediate-grade metamorphic rock.

Metamorphic rocks evolve as temperature and pressure increase. Geologists use a sequence—from the low-grade metamorphosis to the high-grade metamorphosis—to explain how this evolution happens in a particular parent rock. They start with the sedimentary rock shale. Under low temperatures and

DID YOU KNOW?

Shale produces the greatest number of metamorphic rock types.

pressures, shale first morphs into slate. As the temperature and pressure increase, the slate evolves into phyllite, followed by schist, and then gneiss. At higher temperatures and pressures, the gneiss partially melts into another metamorphic rock: migmatite. If the migmatite melts completely, it becomes magma.

If migmatite partially melts, the light-colored minerals collect in the middle of the rock, leaving behind bands of dark-colored, unmelted minerals.

There are many kinds of parent rock, however. So geologists look for certain minerals to determine the conditions that caused metamorphosis in a rock. They call these minerals "index minerals." Just as metamorphic rocks evolve, these minerals evolve as pressure and temperature increase. Under low temperatures and pressures, clay minerals morph into chlorite. As temperature and pressure increase, chlorite changes into biotite, then garnet, staurolite, kyanite, and finally sillimanite. Finding these minerals in metamorphic rock tells geologists about the type and intensity of metamorphic change that the parent rock went through.

A large outcrop of Manhattan schist can be seen in Central Park in New York City.

Grouping Metamorphic Rocks

METAMORPHIC ROCKS ARE DIFFICULT to sort into groups. They form from many kinds of igneous, sedimentary, and metamorphic parent rocks. Any of the parent rocks can undergo many combinations of heat, pressure, and exposure to chemicals in fluids. To begin sorting out the kinds of metamorphic rocks, geologists look at the texture of the rock.

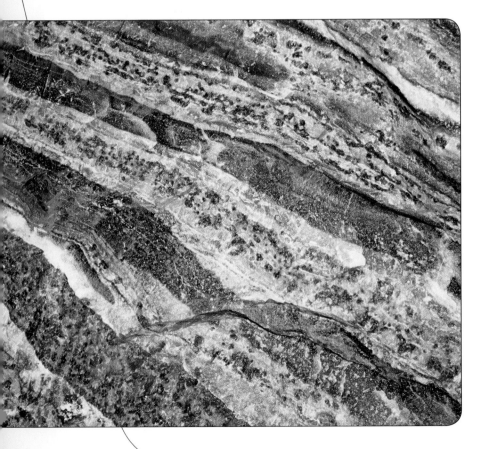

Skarn, a type of metamorphic rock, often contains deposits of metals, such as copper, lead, and gold.

The texture of some metamorphic rock can be different from the texture of the parent rock. The texture of a rock depends on the size of its mineral grains, how close together the grains are, and the orientation of the grains, or how they are lined up. Changes in texture occur because of processes called compaction and recrystallization.

Because of compaction, some metamorphic rocks are denser and more compact than the parent rocks. Great pressure pushes the mineral grains closer together or flattens them, forming a metamorphic rock with patterns of bands or layers. The pressure also makes the metamorphic rock heavier and denser than the original rock.

Because of recrystallization, the mineral crystals change. Crystals are structures that form when atoms line up in three-dimensional patterns. When recrystallization occurs, small crystals in the original rock fuse together to create large crystals of metamorphic rock.

Some metamorphic rocks contain different minerals from those in the parent rocks. The new minerals form because of hydrothermal metamorphism.

Geologists have come up with two major groupings for metamorphic rocks based on texture. One group is called foliates and the other is called nonfoliates.

FOLIATES

Foliated metamorphic rocks are made of two or more minerals. In foliates, the mineral grains line up in one direction. The grains form layers or sheets. Some of the best-known foliated metamorphic rocks are slate, schist, and gneiss. Slate is a low-grade metamorphic rock that forms from shale or mudstone, both sedimentary rocks. Shale is dark colored, usually gray or black, and contains clay minerals. Under increasing pressure and temperature, the clay in the shale becomes unstable. Like

Because slate has excellent cleavage—the ability to break into thin sheets—it is commonly used to create shingles for roofs.

rocks, minerals change when there is a change in the conditions under which they form. The clay minerals recrystallize to form chlorite, a mineral that forms in thin sheets like biotite and muscovite. The lining up of the flat chlorite grains gives slate its foliated texture.

Schist, a medium-grade metamorphic rock, has a shiny look because of light reflecting off the flat mica flakes. The new minerals—such as quartz, feldspar, biotite, and amphibole— grow from the chlorite crystals that recrystallize at the higher temperatures and pressures.

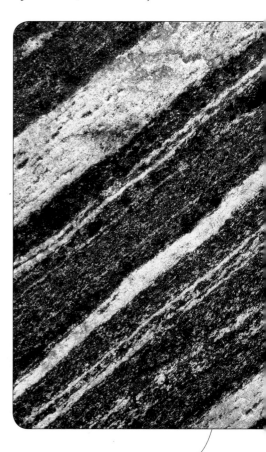

The high-grade metamorphic rock gneiss has large, coarse mineral grains arranged in colored bands. High pressures and temperatures separate light minerals from dark minerals creating the bands. Under some conditions, the parent rock is igneous rock, such as granite. Under other conditions, the parent rock is sedimentary rock, such as shale.

Unlike other types of foliate rocks, gneiss does not easily break into layers.

NONFOLIATES

In nonfoliate—or granular—rocks, mineral grains are not organized in any particular way. These rocks have a grainy texture. Most nonfoliate metamorphic rocks contain one mineral. The best-known nonfoliate rocks are quartzite, marble, and hornfels. Quartzite and marble can form under a wide range of temperatures and pressures. Hornfels can have several minerals. It forms from shale through contact metamorphism.

Quartzite forms from quartz sandstone that has been buried deep in Earth's crust under many layers of sedimentary rock. The high temperatures or high pressure of Earth's interior fuses the quartz crystals in sandstone, forming the larger grains of quartzite. Quartzite is normally white or gray, but impurities can add other colors, such as red and purple.

Hornfels that has a dark appearance contains a large amount of the mineral mica.

Marble forms from the sedimentary rocks limestone or dolomite. These rocks become buried deep within Earth where there are high pressures and high temperatures. Marble forms when heat and pressure cause minerals that make up these rocks to recrystallize. The crystals of the mineral calcite make pure, white marble look like sugar. Other minerals can give marble colors, such as pink or green. Impurities often look like colored veins running through the marble.

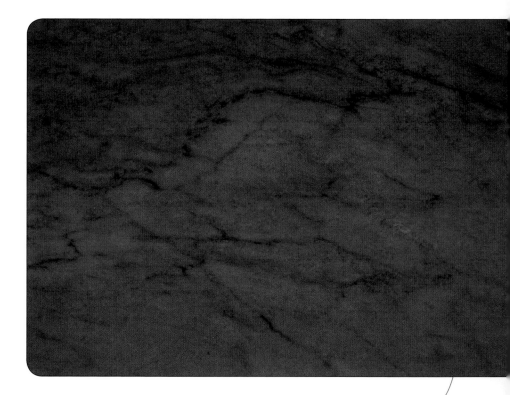

Red marble streaked with blue or black impurities can resemble human skin.

Reading Metamorphic Rocks

Geologists can study metamorphic rocks to learn about the history of Earth. They can tell what kind of metamorphism the parent rock underwent. They can learn about the movement of tectonic plates in the area. They can find out what parent rock the metamorphic rock came from.

A deposit of slate means that the area underwent low-grade metamorphism that acted upon a shale parent rock. The parent rock was made from sediment that was once deposited in a body of water. Finding gneiss, however, means that temperatures and pressures in the area were once very high. The gneiss may have formed because giant tectonic plates collided millions of years ago, forming mountains. If a rock is quartzite, the geologists know that the parent rock was quartz sandstone. This, in turn, shows that the area might once have been the bottom of a sea covered with sediments that came from an ancient granite mountain because of weathering.

Strata in a cliff containing marble, schist, and gneiss in the Sequoia National Forest in California

Digging and Using Metamorphic Rock

ALTHOUGH METAMORPHIC ROCK formed deep within the Earth, forces of nature exposed deposits of the rock millions of years later. Movements of tectonic plates pushed the layers of rocks toward the surface. Erosion by wind, water, and ice scraped layers of sedimentary rock off of the metamorphic rock layers.

Outcroppings are places where marble, shale, and other metamorphic rocks poke out of the ground. After people discovered outcroppings, they began to dig deeper into the metamorphic deposits. The places where coal and other mineral resources are dug out of the ground are called mines. Places where other kinds of rock are dug out are usually known as quarries.

Anthracite, or hard coal, is a metamorphic rock. It

An estimated 7 billion tons (6.3 billion metric tons) of anthracite that can be mined is located in a northeastern area of Pennsylvania known as the Coal Region.

formed from pressure on deposits of bituminous coal, or soft coal. Bituminous coal is a sedimentary rock. Almost all the anthracite in the United States comes from mines in eastern Pennsylvania.

In some places, the anthracite deposits lie deep underground and must be reached through mine shafts or tunnels dug into the sides of mountains. In other places, the deposits are close to Earth's surface. In surface mines, or open-pit mines, power shovels and huge power scoops scrape away the sedimentary rock and dig up the anthracite. Anthracite gives off a great deal of heat and was once widely used in homes and factories. It also gives off fewer pollutants than bituminous coal.

Some marble quarries are on the surface. Others are underground. Because marble breaks easily, great care must be taken when removing this rock from a quarry. Long ago, workers pounded wooden pegs into natural cracks in the marble. They poured water on the pegs to make the wood swell. The swelling wood split off big blocks of marble.

Today workers drill holes in a section of the marble deposit. Through the holes, they thread a special wire cable fitted with industrial diamonds. Diamond is the hardest substance known and can easily cut marble. The cable, operated by a high-speed electric motor, cuts out big blocks of marble. Power saws cut the marble blocks into smaller pieces. The marble is then ready to be carved and used for countertops, statues, tabletops, or fancy flooring or wall covering.

Heavy machinery, such as loaders, carefully moves the large blocks of marble once they have been removed from the quarry.

Is It Marble?

Sculptors prize pure marble, which is white, because of the way light travels through its polished surface. It looks as though you can see down into the stone. Stores, however, sell marble products in many colors. Marble often has a pattern of swirling lines called veins. You can buy a green marble sink, gray or black marble floor tiles, or a red marble countertop.

The colors and patterns in natural marble come from impurities in the marble. Dark marble contains the dark-

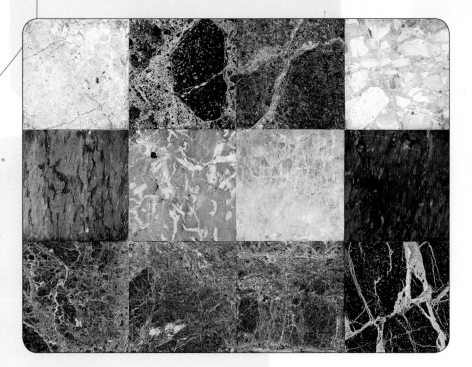

Marble tiles and veins come in a variety of colors depending on each rock's impurities.

colored element carbon, the main element in coal. The metal iron gives marble a pink or red color. Green marble contains the mineral serpentine.

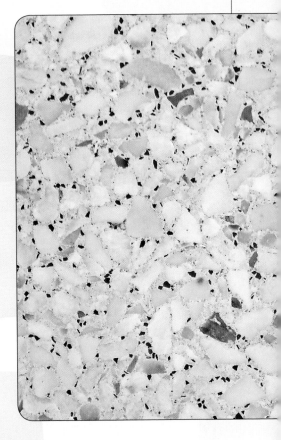

Not all marble colors are created by natural impurities, however. Marble can be dyed many colors. Some marble is not natural. Manufactured marble is made of minerals that are heated and pressed in a process that is like metamorphosis. Some "marble" is not marble at all. "Cultured marble," which is often used to make sinks, is a plastic material.

Marble powder and marble chips are used to create a material called terrazzo. The powder and pieces of marble are dyed and held together with cement. Metal strips outline a picture or pattern. In the way crayons are used to color pictures, the marble mixture is set inside the metal strips to give color to the pattern. The floor is then polished to a high gloss.

Terrazzo floors are less expensive than marble tiles or slabs.

OTHER METAMORPHIC ROCKS

Gneiss, slate, schist, quartzite, and other types of metamorphic rock are also taken from quarries. For example, there are many slate quarries in Great Britain. Slate can either be quarried from deposits near the surface or removed farther underground using tunnels dug into mountainsides. The slate breaks into many small pieces that can be used as crushed stone for roads. Large blocks of slate taken from the quarry are split into sheets. The sheets are then cut into squares and rectangles by power saws.

Slate taken from quarries can be used for roofing and flagstones because the rock is weatherproof and durable.

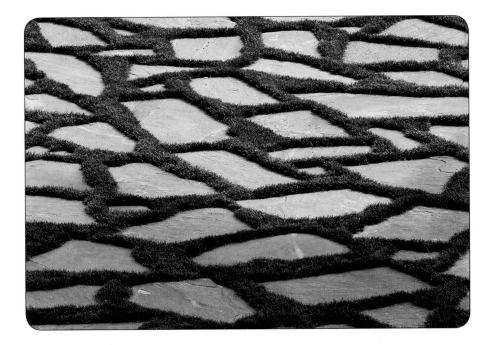

Slate was once a popular material for roofs in North America and Europe. It has largely been replaced by other materials, but it is still used in other parts of the world. Slate is also used for fireplace hearths and garden walkways.

Gneiss is often used as a building material. With its colored bands of red, pink, gray, and black, polished gneiss makes a beautiful stone for decorating the outside of buildings. The semiprecious stone garnet is only found in schist deposits. Jewelers cut and polish garnets for use in rings, necklaces, and other jewelry.

Because slate can be broken into thin, flat slabs, the rocks can be used to decorate a lawn or garden.

People use metamorphic rocks that formed millions of years ago to build roads and buildings. In the form of coal, it is burned for energy in factories and power plants. It also brings art and beauty into our lives in the form of marble statutes and monuments.

Marble is used to make statues not only because it is a strong, beautiful rock, but also because it is resistant to fire.

chemical element—substance made of one type of atom

crust—Earth's thin outer layer of rock

erosion—wearing away of rock or soil by wind, water, or ice

extrusive rocks—rocks made from magma that erupts from volcanoes and cools rapidly; also called volcanic rock

hydrothermal—having to do with hot water

igneous rock—rock formed when magma cools and hardens

intrusive rocks—rocks made from magma that slowly cooled underground; also called plutonic rock

magma—molten rock beneath Earth's crust

mantle—layer of hot rock between Earth's crust and core

marble—common metamorphic rock often used in construction and for carving statues

metamorphic grades—divisions of metamorphic rocks based on the temperature and pressure at which they formed

metamorphosis—changes in composition and texture resulting from heat, pressure, and chemically active gases

quarry—place where stone is dug out of the ground

sedimentary rock—rock formed from the hardening of sediment layers

sediments—small particles of weathered rock

tectonic plates—gigantic pieces of Earth's crust that slide around on magma in the mantle

weathering—breaking down of solid rock into smaller and smaller pieces by wind, water, glaciers, or plant roots

▸ Italian artist and engineer Leonardo da Vinci (1452–1519) invented a machine for cutting marble at marble quarries in Carrara, Italy.

▸ The "lead" in pencils is not lead. In fact, it is not even a metal. It is a metamorphic rock called graphite. Graphite comes from the metamorphosis of soft coal, a sedimentary rock.

▸ The Indian Plate is one of the fastest-moving plates. When it crashed into the Eurasian plate, the collision caused the Himalayas to rise. Formed about 24 million years ago, the Himalayas are the highest and one of the youngest mountain ranges on the planet.

▸ The Tomb of the Unknowns, which contains the remains of unidentified U.S. soldiers who died in World Wars I and II and the Korean War, is made of marble taken from a quarry in Colorado.

The Tomb of the Unknowns is located in Arlington National Cemetery in Virginia.

Further Reading

Ditchfield, Christin. *Coal*. New York: Children's Press, 2002.

Pellant, Chris. *Marble and Other Metamorphic Rocks*. Milwaukee: Gareth Stevens, 2007.

Robson, Pam. *Mountains and Our Moving Earth*. Brookfield, Conn.: Copper Beach Books, 2001.

Stewart, Melissa. *Metamorphic Rocks*. Chicago: Heinemann, 2002.

On the Web

For more information on this topic, use FactHound.
1. Go to *www.facthound.com*
2. Type in this book ID: 0756532558
3. Click on the *Fetch It* button.
FactHound will find the best Web sites for you.

On the Road

The Exploratorium
Metamorphic Mine Exhibit
Gillespie Museum
Stetson University
234 E. Michigan Ave.
DeLand, FL 32723
386/822-7330

Geology Museum
Weeks Hall
University of Wisconsin-Madison
1215 West Dayton St.
Madison, WI 53706
608/262-2399

Explore all the Earth Science books

Erosion: How Land Forms, How It Changes

The Greenhouse Effect: Warming the Planet

Igneous Rocks: From Fire to Stone

Metamorphic Rocks: Recycled Rock

Minerals: From Apatite to Zinc

Natural Resources: Using and Protecting Earth's Supplies

Plate Tectonics: Earth's Moving Crust

Sedimentary Rocks: A Record of Earth's History

Soil: Digging Into Earth's Vital Resource

A complete list of Exploring Science titles is available on our Web site: *www.compasspointbooks.com*